# Vision, Mission, Objectives

**Debra Allcock Tyler**

directory of social change

Published by Directory of Social Change (Registered Charity no. 800517 in England and Wales)

Office: Suite 103, 1 Old Hall Street, Liverpool L3 9HG

Tel: 020 4526 5995

Visit www.dsc.org.uk to find out more about our books, subscription funding website and training events. You can also sign up for e-newsletters so that you're always the first to hear about what's new.

The publisher welcomes suggestions and comments that will help to inform and improve future versions of this and all of our titles. Please give us your feedback by emailing publications@dsc.org.uk.

It should be understood that this publication is intended for guidance only and is not a substitute for professional advice. No responsibility for loss occasioned as a result of any person acting or refraining from acting can be accepted by the author or publisher.

ISBN 978 1 78482 092 3 (print edition)
ISBN 978 1 78482 093 0 (digital edition)


**British Library Cataloguing in Publication Data**
A catalogue record for this book is available from the British Library


Cover and text design by Kate Griffith
Printed and bound in the UK by Martins the Printers, Berwick-upon-Tweed

# Contents

# Introduction

## *Who will this book help?*

This book will help anyone setting up or leading a charity who wants to ensure that their organisation is really making a positive change in the world, but who is struggling to get a clear sense of direction and a set of priorities to achieve that change.

## *What will it give you?*

This book will help you to understand the difference between a vision, a mission and strategic objectives, why each of these concepts matters and how to develop them.

It explains how vision, mission and strategic objectives link to and support each other. It also touches on how to engage people in developing them and how to bring these concepts to life.

# Chapter 1

# Why bother?

*This chapter explains why having a vision, a mission and strategic objectives is worth it.*

Almost all organisations need to have a sense of what they exist for and a plan of how they want to achieve it. The terminology for these things varies from organisation to organisation, but essentially you need to:

- know what it is your organisation is aspiring to achieve in the long term (a vision);
- decide what is the big action that will help you to get there (a mission);
- establish some objectives which will help you to deliver the big actions (strategic objectives).

It really doesn't matter what words you use. If you want to call your vision your purpose, your mission your goal and your strategic objectives your priorities – that's fine. The important thing is that you keep your language consistent and you explain what you mean, so that your key stakeholders (staff, trustees, volunteers, and beneficiaries or service users) are clear what you are referring to you when you use the terms.

When a new registered charity is set up, its founders have to decide which of the 13 'objects' (as defined in the Charities Act 2011) the organisation falls under, such as the advancement of education or the relief of poverty. You can have more than one of these objects.

In your charity's governing document, your object(s) will probably be specified with a little more detail. The overarching object(s) you select will, to a certain extent, describe the vision of your charity – what you are there to achieve.

However, the same 13 legally defined charitable objects apply to thousands of charities. You need to create your own unique vision to describe what it is that your particular charity wants to achieve.

Out of vision, mission and strategic objectives, vision is probably the most important and the hardest thing to get right.

## Why visions matter

Do organisations really need a vision to survive? The short answer to that question is probably not. You could bimble along without a vision, or indeed a mission or strategic objectives – just carrying on with what you have always done and perhaps do a decent job.

But here's the thing: is just bimbling along good enough for you or those you serve? Having a clear sense of direction is consistent with your duty to achieve your charitable objects in service of your beneficiaries, as established in your governing documents. The point of having a vision is so that those who work in your organisation, those who volunteer for it and those who fund it have something to work towards. Something that inspires, generates fresh ideas, encourages positive attitudes to problem solving and makes folk feel that they are working to achieve something that matters. Visions unite people in a common cause. It's the starting point for every other thing you do.

Conversely, in my experience, there is a price to not having a vision – it affects performance. If you just think about your experience with businesses, it is easy to tell when people don't really care about the organisation they are working for – it's just a job. The restaurant where the waiter is busier chatting to the bar staff than serving the customers; the shop where the assistant is on the phone; and so on.

## Symptoms of visionless organisations

- Resistance to change
- Low-level morale
- People give up easily (especially when things go wrong)
- Focus on analysing what went wrong rather than what needs to be done
- Emphasis on internal mechanisms rather than bigger picture
- Focus on staff rather than those the charity is there to serve
- High levels of backbiting and gossip
- Complex and largely unnecessary bureaucracy

# Who is the vision for?

The vision is *not* primarily for the external world. If you are writing your vision thinking about funders or external stakeholders, you're probably starting from the wrong point. It's not a marketing statement or a fundraising pitch. It's for the folk working to deliver the work of the charity – the staff, the volunteers and the trustees – and, ultimately, for your beneficiaries or service users.

Once you get the vision right for the people inside your organisation, then of course you will find ways to make it attractive to funders and supporters (and you will amend marketing and communications materials appropriately). But the vision itself is not for them. It is for you.

Let me be absolutely clear here. Your vision is *not* a marketing strapline. It is your statement of intent not your pitch to punters. For example, DSC's strapline is 'helping you to help others'. It clearly describes what we do and hopefully hooks people in. But our vision is of 'an independent voluntary sector at the heart of social change'. It's not the same thing.

## What does the vision do?

Your vision is the touchstone, the motivating driver, the focus point for people who design the services to help the community or the cause, for those who provide the back office support, for those who raise the money. For those your charity serves, the vision demonstrates what they are part of. It sets the overall context by which individuals can connect with the organisation and help develop its work. Having a clear vision also helps other people to hold you accountable for delivering it. And, above all, it helps you to make sure that the tasks you are carrying out are contributing towards achieving that vision, or shows you when you may be spending your energy on a distraction.

The vision is the primary statement that trustees have to align behind and be committed to achieving. They will hold the staff to account for the delivery of the charity's vision and, in turn, they will be held to account by beneficiaries or service users and other stakeholders. Therefore, it is part of trustees' strategic accountability to ensure that the charity has a clearly articulated and well-understood vision that the staff and volunteers are working towards delivering.

## Whose job is it?

It is important that your vision, mission and strategic objectives are the concern of everyone in the organisation. Your charity's direction should not be seen as something just your board or senior leadership need to worry about. Or as something that your staff should look after on their own. Ultimately, it's everyone's business. However, when developing your vision, mission and strategic objectives, you'll need to make sure the right people are involved at the right stages.

In terms of the vision, it often emerges organically at the time of the charity's inception and goes on to inform which of the 13 legally allowed charitable objects you fall under when the charity is registered.

However, visions do need revisiting to make sure that they are still relevant to the environment in which the charity is now operating and that the language fits a more modern context.

It is vital that trustees are involved in creating the vision as they are accountable for its delivery. Nevertheless, a wise board will understand that it should engage with its staff, volunteers and beneficiary or service user group so that there is a collective ownership of it.

Whereas the board must be involved in vision setting in any charity, when it comes to developing the subsequent mission and strategic objectives, you can do this slightly differently depending on your organisation's size. If your charity is a small one with mostly volunteers, then the work of developing the mission and strategic objectives is probably still that of the board of trustees. However, if yours is a larger charity with paid staff, then the detail of developing the mission and strategic objectives is often best left to the staff team, and it's the job of the trustees to sign off the plan that has been brought to them. Why?

- ■ Staff and volunteers are usually better placed than the board to know what is possible within the context of the charity and its beneficiaries or service users.

- ■ Boards don't meet that often, so it is quite possible they will slow down the development of missions and strategic objectives simply because of diary clashes. If the process takes too long, ideas lose impetus.

- ■ The staff and volunteers have to do the work to deliver the mission and strategic objectives. The board doesn't. It's easier and more motivating to deliver something you have developed yourself rather than something devised by others who are disconnected from the work.

- ■ The board is more likely, and indeed better placed, to be objective in assessing the relative merits of the mission and strategic objectives if trustees weren't involved in creating the details of them.

- ■ The board is also more likely to be objective in monitoring progress against delivery of the mission and strategic objectives if trustees didn't build them themselves.

Having said all that, regardless of who is involved in creating and developing the mission and strategic objectives, the board needs to take ownership of them. I will talk about mission and strategic objectives in more detail in chapters 3 and 4, respectively.

# Chapter 2

# What is a vision?

*This chapter explains what a vision is and what it is not.*

The typical pattern in the voluntary sector is that someone spots an injustice, or has a friend in need, or something bad happens to them or a member of their family, and they decide to set up a charity to do something about it. At this stage, they will almost always have a fairly clear vision of what it is they want to change – although it may not necessarily be clearly articulated.

> 'If you want to build a ship then don't drum up men to gather wood, give orders and divide the work. Rather teach them to yearn for the far and endless sea.'

It may be things like 'I want to get better support for teenagers with cancer', 'I want to stop people abusing animals' or 'I want to find a way to make sure that no one ever goes hungry in my town'. Essentially, what they are describing is the ideal state of affairs if their charity succeeds.

It is rarely articulated in detail, but it's expressed with emotion and passion. Much like the advice in the box on the left, which is derived from the work of Antoine de Saint-Exupéry, French author and aviator, it's a yearning for the far and endless sea.[1]

---

[1] This quote is believed to have been derived from a text in Saint-Exupéry's book *Citadelle* (translated in English as *The Wisdom of the Sands*). Antoine de Saint-Exupéry, *Citadelle*, Paris, Gallimard, 1948, p. 687.

A vision is *not* a list of actions that you take or a description of what your charity does. 'We provide support for women ex-offenders' or 'We support young carers to have lives independent of those they care for' describes what you do – it is *not* a vision.

A vision articulates the end state – what it will look and/or feel like if you do your job well.

This matters, because if your vision describes only what you do, it limits your ability to change your activity in order to achieve that vision. You've confused what you're trying to achieve with what you do, and that's where it's easy to get stuck.

For example, if you believe that providing training in job-hunting skills for women ex-offenders is your end result, rather than a means to achieve your vision, you are more likely to get a bit stuck if suddenly the government starts providing that training – and your particular offering in job-hunting skills is no longer needed.

Whereas if your vision is 'Women ex-offenders leading positive lives', your vision doesn't necessarily have to change as external circumstances do, and you are open to adapting and creating a new offer to those you serve. So, to continue the example, rather than continuing with the training in job-hunting skills, you might start offering life skills or assertiveness programmes in order to help achieve your vision.

> **A vision is:**
>
> A clear idea of what the world will look like when your organisation's purpose is achieved. For example:
>
> 'Women ex-offenders leading positive lives'
>
> 'Young carers living a life of their own'

## Creating a vision

There is a tendency to both oversimplify and overcomplicate the creation of a vision. You can oversimplify the process by thinking that you don't need to go to all the trouble of consulting people and that it's easier to just get a small group of people to produce a vision and tell others what it is. And you can overcomplicate the vision by using clever-sounding language or trying to describe everything you do, thereby ending up with several paragraphs rather than one clear sentence.

A vision that is longer than one sentence (or even worse, goes on for several paragraphs) isn't particularly inspiring. If it doesn't trip off the tongue easily, it won't be remembered.

Don't fall into the trap of thinking that 'big' words will make your vision better. 'Our vision is to achieve a socially coherent, economically vibrant community which minimises social exclusion and enables the co-creation and co-production of community critical services to prevent the proliferation of exclusion-related crime and misdemeanours' might sound clever but does the opposite of inspire!

Funnily enough, it's the process of consulting that often ends up producing waffly, meaningless visions. You might think that consulting means you have to satisfy everyone, so you try to incorporate all the words suggested and very likely end up with gibberish.

But without consulting you won't end up with buy-in – and your vision will not be as strong – so the pros of consulting definitely outweigh the cons.

## Characteristics of strong visions

- They are inspiring
- They are believable – they fit the context of the organisation
- They feel achievable, even if not in this lifetime
- They are rarely longer than 7–10 words
- They are memorable
- They use simple everyday language that people can understand and identify with
- They describe a vision of the future
- They stand the test of time – they are usually big enough to cope with a changing external environment
- Staff, trustees, volunteers and beneficiaries or service users have been involved in creating them

# Process for creating a vision

## *Stage 1 – Buy into the concept of vision*

- Have a conversation with the board about the need for a new/revamped/revised vision.
- Ask:
  - ❑ What is our vision currently?
  - ❑ Is it still relevant?
  - ❑ Do we all buy into it?
  - ❑ Is it serving us?
  - ❑ What key words describe what we are trying to do/achieve?

## *Stage 2 – Consult (round one)*

- Gather your teams (staff, volunteers and beneficiaries or service users, where appropriate) together and ask:
  - ❑ What is special about our organisation?
  - ❑ What do we want to achieve?
  - ❑ Who are we trying to serve?
  - ❑ What will the world look like for our beneficiaries or service users if we are so successful that we're no longer needed?
  - ❑ What key words describe what we are trying to do/achieve?

> **Top tip**
>
> Remember that the more you can involve staff, trustees, volunteers and beneficiaries or service users in creating your vision, the more buy-in and commitment you will get to delivering the actions you need to achieve it.

## *Stage 3 – Come up with a statement*

- Ask a small group, which includes a trustee, staff member, executive team member and beneficiary or service user, to go away and incorporate the key words that have come up from your consultations into a statement.

- Avoid phrases like 'we will' or 'we aim to' – you don't need them. Create a simple statement of what the world will look like if you achieve your purpose.

> **Top tip**
>
> Focus on the spirit of your vision statement, not the specific words.

- Group words which are essentially similar in intent (such as integrity, trust and honesty) and agree on one word which encapsulates all of them for you.

- Settle on a few key words that must appear in the vision.

- Come up with a sentence (no more than 7–10 words if possible) behind which you can align.

## *Stage 4 – Consult (round two)*

- Share what you have come up with your staff, trustees, volunteers and beneficiaries or service users.

- Ask them how the statement you created makes them feel.

- Avoid getting into debates about specific words – it's not about the words but what the statement envisions for them.

## *Stage 5 – Communicate, communicate, communicate*

- Make sure you are communicating the vision regularly in one-to-ones, board meetings and team meetings.

- Include it in every formal team briefing.

- When reporting results internally or to funders, link what you've done to the vision.

> **Top tip**
> Ask for alignment behind the vision rather than agreement. Agreement means people have to change their minds, which is hard for folk to do, whereas alignment means they can keep their view but still get behind the vision.

- In appraisals and one-to-ones, link individuals' work to the delivery of the vision.
- In your annual report and accounts, link what you have done to the vision.
- Remind folk of the vision regularly.

By the way, this five-step process of building a vision is also a good template for creating your mission and strategic objectives. You'll need to adapt it, obviously, but the main principles remain the same.

## The Moses test

One of my favourite analogies for knowing if your vision is a strong one is the story of Moses, which appears in the ancient texts of three of the major religions: Judaism, Christianity and Islam.

### Moses' story

According to the scriptures, the daughter of the Egyptian Pharoah adopted a boy called Moses. He was brought up as her son but one day discovered that he was actually the son of a Jewish slave. Most of the Jews in Egypt at the time were slaves. When Moses grew up, he decided that he wanted to lead the Jewish people to a land where they would be free. It took a bit of convincing, hence Moses had to come up with a vision of 'a land of milk and honey' to show them the perilous journey was worth it. The Pharaoh wasn't happy about his main workforce leaving and tried to prevent it. Even after God did a bit of smiting of the Egyptians by sending plagues and other problems, the Pharaoh still pursued the Jews to the Red Sea. God parted the Red Sea so Moses and his people could get away, and they started their journey towards the land of milk and honey.

What is so powerful about Moses' vision is its simplicity – 'a land of milk and honey'.

Compare it with the sort of vision which we might have come up with today – full of jargon and clever-sounding words that basically confuse rather than inspire. Today, Moses' vision would probably read something like this: 'To navigate disadvantaged and dislocated beneficiaries to an as yet unspecified geographical area that contains sustainable sources of bovine lactate and apiary produce in order to promote the economic, physical and spiritual regeneration of the dispossessed slaves of Egypt.' Bleuch!

### The Moses test

This is the final step to make sure the statement you've come up with is definitely the best vision you can create. If the answer to all of the following questions is yes, you've done it!

- ❏ Does your vision energise and motivate people?
- ❏ Is it credible and easy for folk to get behind?
- ❏ Can it be fulfilled successfully (at any stage in the future)?
- ❏ Is it shorter than ten words?
- ❏ Will it stick in people's minds?
- ❏ Is it framed in understandable and familiar language?
- ❏ Does it paint a picture of your ideal version of the future?
- ❏ Will it remain equally relevant with time, as your organisation and external circumstances change?

Overleaf are some examples of visions for fictional charities that were developed by charity staff members who attended a series of programmes I was running about developing visions. I think these broadly pass the Moses test.

**Pre-school Play Association**

*Confident, happy children*

**Voluntary Services International**

*A world at peace*

**Education and Care Centre**

*A future for young people with a past*

**Welcome Asylum Seeker Support Group**

*Safely at home in a welcoming city*

**Young Single Homeless Project**

*Yooves with rooves*

**Age Care**

*Sex and sangria for senior citizens*

# Chapter 3

# What is a mission?

*This chapter explains what a mission is and what it is not.*

You may be familiar with the famous words spoken by John F. Kennedy, President of the United States. In a speech in 1961 he said: 'I believe that this nation should commit itself to achieving the goal, before this decade is out, of landing a man on the moon and returning him safely to the earth.'[2]

This is often paraphrased as 'a man on the moon by the end of the decade' and noted as an example of a powerful vision. But, actually, this isn't really a vision – it's more of a mission (also referred to as an aim). Technically speaking, the vision, if it had been articulated at the time, would more likely have been 'humankind in space'.

A mission is, essentially, the single big goal that is going to help you to achieve your vision. So 'a man on the moon by the end of the decade' is the big audacious goal which helps to achieve 'humankind in space'. It is measurable in some way – a man, the moon, the end of the decade – which visions typically aren't. But it is equally simple and easy to understand.

It has been my experience that missions can be incredibly hard to create – sometimes even harder than visions – usually because they're about making big choices on which folk often won't agree.

---

[2] President John F. Kennedy, speech to Congress, 25 May 1961, Section IX: Space, www.nasa.gov/vision/space/features/jfk_speech_text.html, accessed 17 December 2021.

Missions will always link to the vision and be a clear step towards achieving it.

## Creating a mission

The process of creating a mission really comes down to debating what the big priority is – what is the biggest thing you can do that will help you to achieve your vision? You will often have choices here, as there will be different activities that you can focus on in order to get the job done. This is likely to generate a lot of discussion, since not everyone will agree on which the most important activity is.

Just like when creating your vision, you will need to engage your staff, trustees, volunteers and beneficiaries or service users in debate. The process of engaging them will be very similar to that you used to determine your vision (see page 13) – simply follow the same basic guidelines.

You will need to make it clear that a decision on a single mission will have to be made – and, honestly, I'd be inclined to avoid compromising by having lots of missions to keep folk happy. Much better to settle on one pretty big one. Otherwise, you make it harder for people to know what to prioritise, and it stretches resources in too many directions.

Also, as you'll see in the next chapter, sometimes what people think of as missions can actually be expressed as strategic objectives – so you can win any mission 'battles' that way.

**Top tip**

Don't over-wordsmith your mission. Try not to think of it as a statement but more as a big action to achieve.

Start drafting your mission by asking questions such as:

- What is the single biggest action we could take which will move us closer to achieving our vision?
- What feels like an achievable timescale?
- What feels big, but not so big that we can't see ourselves achieving it?
- What can we start straight away?

Once the mission has been achieved, a new mission becomes necessary – the next big goal towards achieving your charity's vision.

So, we got a man on the moon, now we want to visit Mars – the next big mission towards achieving the vision of 'humankind in space'.

Using my delegates in the previous chapter as an example, we might have:

**Pre-school Play Association**

*Vision: Confident, happy children*

*Mission: By end of 2025, to have placed 50% of all eligible children in our catchment area in appropriate pre-school play environment*

**Voluntary Services International**

*Vision: A world at peace*

*Mission: To have placed volunteers in 90 countries by 2030*

**Education and Care Centre**

*Vision: A future for young people with a past*

*Mission: By 2026, to have secured £250,000 of funding to develop an outreach counselling service*

**Welcome Asylum Seeker Support Group**

*Vision: Safely at home in a welcoming city*

*Mission: To have secured houses/apartments to provide transitional homes for all newly arrived refugees within two weeks of their arrival*

**Young Single Homeless Project**

*Vision: Yooves with rooves*

*Mission: By 2030, to have raised funds to buy a building that will temporarily accommodate young people transitioning from homelessness to secure housing*

**Age Care**

*Vision: Sex and sangria for senior citizens*

*Mission: By 2025, to have developed a range of outreach social programmes for older folk in our community within three miles of their homes*

# Chapter 4

# What are strategic objectives?

*This chapter explains what strategic objectives are and what they are not.*

A strategic objective is an agreed action that you need to take in order to achieve your mission. It is practical – essentially, it gives you direction about the tasks you need to undertake.

There will usually be more than one strategic objective, and they will be specific, measurable, time bound and describe the work that needs to be done – much as the mission does but with a lot more of them and in slightly more detail.

If you take the example of 'humankind in space' as the vision with 'a man on the moon by the end of the decade' as the mission, then your strategic objectives will be things that help you to land astronauts on the moon such as: develop appropriate rocket fuel, build a spaceship, train astronauts and so on.

Your strategic objectives will usually have specific dates set against them – usually linked to each other. So, for example, you probably need to develop appropriate rocket fuel before you build the spaceship, as you have to build the spaceship to accommodate the fuel. Having said that, many strategic objectives can work concurrently.

I frequently interchange the term 'strategic *objective*' with 'strategic *priority*' – this is to emphasise that the work spent on delivering this is the most important work in the organisation.

## Strategic objectives linked to mission

**Vision:** Women ex-offenders leading positive lives

**Mission:** By 2030, 60% of all women ex-offenders will have attended a programme that enables them to start their own business.

**Strategic objectives:**

1. Design a training programme that teaches entrepreneurship by end of 2022

2. Build a team of trainers who are expert in entrepreneurship by end of 2022

3. Visit all female prisons in the UK to convince the governors to use our entrepreneurship programme as part of their rehabilitation training by June 2025

# Creating strategic objectives

You're probably tired of hearing this now, but you have to consult – again. At this stage, it is less imperative to involve trustees. As strategic objectives concern more operational work, the staff and perhaps your volunteers will be best placed to draft them.

To create the strategic objectives, you should start with your mission and discuss what key relatively short-term actions you can take to achieve it.

Avoid being too detailed. A strategic objective should give you a sense of direction and actions related to delivering it, without being too prescriptive. As with most things, getting hung up on the fine details often doesn't help. The key is to have an idea of what it is you need people to do, establish some parameters around it (your budget and timescales, for example) and then let them get on with it.

The more detailed your strategic plan becomes, the less strategic it is!

## Case study: Another way to develop strategic objectives

The approach outlined in this book is a tried-and-tested way of developing your strategic objectives; however, for those of you ready to try a fresh and more innovative approach, we do it a little differently at DSC. Here's how it works.

We've created a set of strategic priorities which aren't time bound or measurable in and of themselves – that is, we don't have a five-year timescale like others might. Instead, each planning cycle (which for us is yearly) we build our budget and plans around these same priorities.

As per standard practice, our strategic priorities were agreed by our board, and then it was our job to get on with delivering against them.
The priorities are 'to develop our work regionally, to expand our expertise and to build our digital offering'.

Our plans in any given year will detail specific projects or actions to help us move further towards achieving these strategic priorities in that year. For example, our 2019 plan included developing a governance app to help improve charity governance (which covered the digital and expertise aspects of our strategic priorities). This had a budget and a specific plan against it.

So we don't change our strategic priorities but make sure that everything we do each year takes us closer to achieving them (and our mission and vision). This approach makes us more responsive to our environment.

Strategic objectives are more flexible than the vision or mission. You will meet obstacles along the way and need to change what you do. The developers of rocket fuel had to explore different accelerants and versions of hydrogen, for example, before they came up with the perfect combination. They faced setbacks and delays just as we all do.

Too detailed and specific an objective can drive organisations to delivering against the plan rather than achieving that objective. It removes the possibility of flexing and doing something different to get the same result. In other words, you're forgetting the end goal because you're so focused on what the plan said.

Your strategic objectives are more like a handrail than a handcuff. They are there to help you to plan and prioritise what actions you need to be taking in any given period, but you should still accept that you will need to be flexible. Once you start work towards your strategic objectives, it is still possible that circumstances will change and you will need to change what you do.

To continue the thread, here's the final set of vision, mission and strategic objectives (invented by me purely for illustrative purposes) for the organisations shared in the previous chapters.

**Pre-school Play Association**

*Vision: Confident, happy children*

*Mission: By end 2025, to have placed 50% of all eligible children in our catchment area in appropriate pre-school play environment*

*Strategic objectives:*

1   *Seek funding of £70,000 spread over three years to recruit a trainer to train new pre-school support workers by March 2022*
2   *Establish a network of existing pre-school play associations in the catchment area by August 2022*

3    Commission research into how many children in our catchment area are eligible – to be completed by January 2023

## Voluntary Services International

*Vision: A world at peace*

*Mission: To have placed volunteers in 90 countries by 2030*

*Strategic objectives:*

1    Connect with the embassies in 50% of the target countries by end of 2022 to establish the links for support
2    Recruit 50 country managers by end of 2023
3    Recruit a minimum of ten volunteers per country by 2024

## Education and Care Centre

*Vision: A future for young people with a past*

*Mission: By 2026, to have secured £250,000 of funding to develop an outreach counselling service*

*Strategic objectives:*

1    Recruit three specialist fundraisers to cover companies, trusts and foundations and major donors by June 2022
2    Identify five core communities most in need by June 2022
3    Recruit ten part-time counsellors from within the five identified communities by December 2022

## Welcome Asylum Seeker Support Group

*Vision: Safely at home in a welcoming city*

*Mission: To have secured houses/apartments to provide transitional homes for all newly arrived refugees within two weeks of their arrival*

*Strategic objectives:*

1  *To cost the houses and apartments needed and begin a capital campaign to either buy or lease by September 2022*
2  *To engage local partners in developing post-homing support services for refugees and their families by December 2023*

## Young Single Homeless Project

*Vision: Yooves with rooves*

*Mission: By 2025, to have raised funds to buy a building that will temporarily accommodate young people transitioning from homelessness to secure housing*

*Strategic objective:*

1  *Source and cost an appropriate building and develop a capital appeal – begin January 2022 with aim for full funding by January 2024*

## Age Care

*Vision: Sex and sangria for senior citizens*

*Mission: By 2025, to have developed a range of outreach social programmes for older folk in our community within three miles of their homes*

*Strategic objectives:*

1  *To research and analyse how many older folk qualify for outreach work by March 2022*
2  *To recruit programme developers to begin the design of the work by December 2022*
3  *To beta test the prototype programmes on a series of focus groups between January 2023 and September 2023*

# Chapter 5

# Bringing it to life

*This chapter talks about how to bring your vision, mission and strategic objectives to life.*

No matter how powerful or well-crafted you think your vision, mission and strategic objectives are, you will struggle to deliver them unless you bring these ideas to life, so that people feel connected and engaged with them.

Very often organisations do the work creating the vision, mission and strategic objectives, write it all up and then consign it to a drawer to be brought out once a quarter to report to trustees on performance against the plan. Frequently, such reporting back focuses on progress against the more detailed plan (the strategic objectives) rather than on how well things are moving towards achieving the wider vision or mission. However, the more detailed plan is only there to help achieve the mission and vision. It is too easy to forget the bigger picture or the purpose of it all if you don't constantly remind people of the context.

So if you want to achieve all the benefits of having a well-thought-through vision with a powerful mission and achievable strategic objectives, then you have to bring it all to life. It needs to be something that your staff and volunteers have in their minds as they go about their work.

How do you make that happen? There are two simple steps: brief it and bring it to life.

## Brief it

Don't make the mistake of thinking that you can just write it all down in a document and send it round to folks. The reality is that most people won't read it. If you're lucky, some might skim it through; others will place it straight into a drawer or their 'Things to get round to reading' folder.

To counteract this, you need to plan and schedule briefing meetings with your staff, volunteers and other key stakeholders to explain the vision, mission and strategic objectives to them.

If your organisation is larger and has lots of staff, then you will probably start by briefing your leadership team and then get them to cascade the information down through the organisation.

The key thing is to make sure that your leadership team are committed to and engaged by the vision, mission and strategic objectives so that they can brief with conviction and passion. So this isn't something that can be rushed. You need to create plenty of time for discussion about how to brief well, think about any questions that might be asked and decide on the key messages that you want people to take away.

Some things to remember:

- It's not about being able to recite the vision, mission and strategic objectives verbatim. If people really understand what these things mean for your organisation, they will be able to give the gist of them in such a way that they are easily understood.

- Briefing once will not be enough. You will need to make sure that all three concepts are built into your monthly reporting, your quarterly reports to the board and whatever other regular communication mechanisms you use.


## Bring it to life

It's not enough to tell people what the vision, mission and strategic objectives are. You need to speak them into life by demonstrating – through your tone and body language – how excited you are about them.

Getting people engaged is relatively easy to do when it comes to your strategic objectives. This is because, typically, they translate to some specific targets or actions that each department has to deliver.

The challenge is making every member of your organisation understand how their efforts are helping to deliver the vision and mission. Both of these concepts may feel more remote, especially for those who would consider themselves to be 'back office' workers. More importantly, you need to find a way to translate them into something relevant for their department or role. By bringing your vision and mission to life in your staff's daily work, you help to keep the focus on the big picture and give yourself a better chance of actually achieving what your organisation is there for.

You need to work with your leadership team and managers to help them find a way to illustrate what delivery of the vision and mission looks like for their departments. For example, DSC's vision is of 'an independent voluntary sector at the heart of social change', our mission is 'to be an agent connecting givers, influencers and service deliverers' and our strategic objectives are framed around extending our reach regionally and digitally, and enhancing our expertise.

At DSC, we bring these elements to life and make them relevant to staff by talking about how the work that they do directly helps us to achieve our vision, mission and strategic objectives. For example, the finance team have to pay invoices for the venues we use to deliver training. Any time they process and pay invoices on time, that means there is a space available for our trainers to deliver courses in, say, fundraising strategy. When charities get that training, they are able to raise more money for their work. This means that a child with a disability gets a wheelchair; a victim of domestic violence has a refuge to go to; a parent who has lost a child has access to a counselling service – none of which would be possible if the charity hadn't come to a venue to attend our training to learn how to raise money. The finance team's work enables the charities we serve to do their work better, which attracts more people to ask for our help, which increases our reach and, ultimately, the charities we help are helping to make society better.

You can take what seems like a mundane routine job and show how it's relevant to your vision and, by doing that, breathe life and energy into it. And if you can do that with a finance team, imagine how much easier it is to achieve this for fundraisers, front-line workers or volunteers, where they can see at first hand the impact of their work.

Remember that your vision, mission and strategic objectives are pretty much useless if they stay on paper rather than becoming part of your organisation's day-to-day life. So take the time to find ways to translate them into something that staff and volunteers can easily relate to, understand and feel energised and enthused by.